Sapphire:
A Life That Almost Wasn't

Lorrie Blitch

Illustrated By: Mark Ruben Abacajan

Order this book online at www.trafford.com
or email orders@trafford.com

Most Trafford titles are also available at major online book retailers.

© Copyright 2015 Lorrie Blitch.

All rights reserved. No part of this publication may be reproduced, stored in a retrieval system, or transmitted, in any form or by any means, electronic, mechanical, photocopying, recording, or otherwise, without the written prior permission of the author.

Print information available on the last page.

ISBN: 978-1-4907-6345-3 (sc)
ISBN: 978-1-4907-6346-0 (e)

Library of Congress Control Number: 2015916568

Because of the dynamic nature of the Internet, any web addresses or links contained in this book may have changed since publication and may no longer be valid. The views expressed in this work are solely those of the author and do not necessarily reflect the views of the publisher, and the publisher hereby disclaims any responsibility for them.

Our mission is to efficiently provide the world's finest, most comprehensive book publishing service, enabling every author to experience success. To find out how to publish your book, your way, and have it available worldwide, visit us online at www.trafford.com

Any people depicted in stock imagery provided by Thinkstock are models,
and such images are being used for illustrative purposes only.
Certain stock imagery © Thinkstock.

Trafford rev. 10/07/2015

 www.trafford.com

North America & international
toll-free: 1 888 232 4444 (USA & Canada)
fax: 812 355 4082

Each life has a purpose, is precious, significant and adds value to this world and to the lives of others. That value is immeasurable and can be manifested in many ways that will help the life of another person from a smile, to a kind word, advice, a comforting touch or the saving of another life. We will all know one day why each life is on this earth, but in the mean time, it is our responsibility to care and protect each life as if it were our own. I hope that you enjoy this book as much as I have enjoyed writing it.

Dedicated to all pets who bring so much joy to our lives

It was a cold windy night with temperatures well into the thirties. The cold temperature was not typical for this time of year, thought the janitor as he made his nightly trip to the trash bin behind The Magellan Academy. He had been cleaning the private school for a little over a year and his nights had been routine and uneventful. However, tonight was to be different from other nights.

Walking to the large trash bin, he could feel the cold wind cut through his jacket that chilled him to the bone. Opening the gate to the trash bin brought to his nose that familiar smell. The trash bin was large, cold, and dark. He opened the lid and began pouring the contents of the activities of the students for the day into the large dark cold bin. "Mew! Mew! Mew!"

He stopped pouring the contents into the trash bin. What was that sound? Where was it coming from? "Mew! Mew! Mew!" He listened intently. A cold silence with only the rustling of the trees all around him enveloped the moment. He no longer heard the faint noise. Had he imagined it? He continued emptying the trash containers into the bin. "Mew! Mew! Mew!"

He again stopped emptying the trash cans. "Mew! Mew! Mew!" The weak sound was close. "Mew! Mew! Mew!" He could hear the faint noise, but could not locate the sound. "Mew! Mew! Mew!" Perplexed, he looked over, under, and around the trash bin. "Mew! Mew! Mew!" Where was the sound coming from? The rustling of the leaves on the trees prevented him from locating the sound. He turned and walked outside the gate. "Mew! Mew! Mew!"

He could not get the sound out of his head. He turned and walked back to the gates and entered where the cold dark trash cans stood. "Mew! Mew! Mew!" The sound was closer and a little louder this time. He turned his ear towards the noise. "Mew! Mew! Mew!" The sound would not stop this time as if to signal the janitor that he should not leave. He looked inside the large dark cold trash bins. "Mew! Mew! Mew!" The sounds now took on a different tone: One of desperation. He looked left and right and noted that the sound was louder from his right. As he rummaged through the trash he saw a small taped cardboard box. He found it! This is where the noise was coming from.

He picked up the box and a slight movement was felt from inside. The sounds were faint but constant. He carried the box back to The Magellan Academy. Inside, the school nurse and the school administrator were completing their chores. The janitor walked quickly into the nurse's office. In a hurried excited voice he exclaimed, "Look! I found this sealed box in the trash bin and it is making noises."

As the nurse and school administrator opened the sealed cardboard box, the lives of two little tiny kittens unfolded. The janitor asked, "How old do you think they are?" The nurse replied, "Probably a day old. Look, their eyes are still closed from birth." The school administrator picked up one of the kittens, so small that they comfortably in the palm of her hand. Both kittens were cold and shook like leaves on a tree from the cold night air. "These kittens would not have lasted the night in this temperature, said the nurse. "Who would do such a horrible thing to a little innocent life?" remarked the administrator.

The shivering, hungry and tired kittens looked up with their closed eyes desperate for affection, food, and warmth. Concerned that the kittens would not survive much longer, the school administrator quickly ran to the kitchen and warmed towels and milk in the microwave. The school nurse pondered how the kittens could be fed. "Ah ha. I've got it. We can use a syringe from my clinic to feed them." The school administrator returned with the warm towels and warm milk. She gently wrapped both kittens in the warm towels. The nurse and administrator filled two syringes with milk and feed the little kittens. The kittens liked the touch of their new human parents.

The kittens drank so much warm milk that their bellies were bulging. The administrator warmed more towels and placed them in the small container. The kittens stopped shivering and fell asleep. A sigh of relief came upon everyone. The nurse pondered all options and stated, "Now what do we do with them? We cannot leave them here alone. They have to be fed and kept warm." The administrator stated "I suppose that I will take them home, feed them and keep them warm until the morning." The administrator picked up the container with the sleeping kittens and walked out the door into the cold windy night air. The kittens did not move as their bellies were full and the warm towels enveloped them.

The kittens were gently placed in the car for the drive home. The administrator thought about the reaction her pet cat, Cashmir, would have towards the little kittens. He was not a cat to share his home or his human family with anyone. Cashmir disliked intruders of any kind into his home.

The administrator arrived home and as she picked up the little container with the kittens, she heard a faint, "Mew! Mew! Mew!" Hummm. Maybe the towels were no longer warm enough; maybe they were hungry or didn't like to be moved since their bellies were so full. Upon opening the front door she was greeted by her cat, Cashmir. He immediately became suspicious when he heard the sounds coming from the container. Inquisitive, he began sniffing the small box. Suddenly, a loud hiss erupted from Cashmir. Quickly, the administrator placed the kittens in a room to and turned up the heat.

The towels were heated and the kittens were again fed warm milk. The kittens fell asleep once again. Tired from the long day, the administrator climbed into bed and fell into a deep slumber. "Mew! Mew! Mew!" The administrator woke up and looked at the clock. It was midnight. "Mew! Mew! Mew!" The sound wouldn't stop. She made her way into the room where she placed the kittens. She opened the door to find the kittens awake stretching upward with eyes closed. Cashmir, curious of the kittens began to hiss at the sound of the kittens. "Cashmir!" exclaimed the administrator, "Be nice. They are little kittens that need our help." She warmed the towels again and placed the kittens in the towels. This did not calm the kittens. "Awwww ha." They must be hungry. Once again the little kittens were fed and they fell into a deep slumber. Again at 2:00 am, at 4:00 am, and then at 6:00 am the little kittens woke up to be fed.

VETERINARY OFFICE

Tired from the long night of every two hours feedings, the administrator dressed and took the kittens to the vet for an examination. Upon arrival to the vet, the tiny little kittens were taken from the box and placed on the scales individually. Each tiny kitten fit into each hand of the administrator. Both kittens were two ounces apiece. The veterinarian said that both kittens would be fine, but would need to be fed every two hours and kept at a constant 99 degrees. The administrator sighed, but knew that the kittens were worth every bit of care they needed, after all, they are a life and their life has value.

Days turned into weeks and weeks turned into months and eventually the tiny kittens were weaned from their bottle onto regular kitten food. Both were litter trained. The kittens were then named, Sapphire and Stewart.

Once Sapphire and Stewart were grown, trained and had all their shots, this marked the period when a home was to be found for them. Stewart was quickly adopted by a Magellan Academy teacher; however, Sapphire was a special needs cat. She was blind. No one seemed to be interested in adopting Sapphire. She waited and waited for a new home, but no one was interested. After several months of waiting for adoption, the administrator decided to adopt Sapphire into her home.

A challenge awaited as Cashmir had to accept a new cat into his home. Cashmir, as to be expected, was upset and jealous of a new cat in his home. He hissed and growled at Sapphire. His feelings towards the administrator were angry as if to say, "How could you allow another cat to invade my home?" Eventually, Cashmir did accept Sapphire and they have many happy days playing and chasing each other.

Since Sapphire was blind, she faced challenges to find her way around her new home that had many rooms and stairs. Blindness did not hold Sapphire back; she found her way throughout her new home with the help of her new owner. She frequently spends many hours snuggled on a bed or in the enclosed outside porch. She is a very content and happy cat that has brought so much joy to her new owners. Her life is invaluable.

CPSIA information can be obtained
at www.ICGtesting.com
Printed in the USA
LVHW070732040119
602590LV00019B/1396/P